# Out of Your Tree 2

I dedicate this book to the memory of Mark Spellman
from Dalkey, County Dublin
who died tragically at the age of 26.

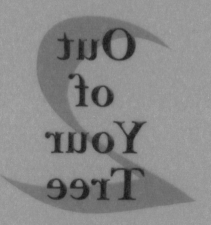

# Out of Your Tree

I dedicate this book to the memory of Mark Spellman
from Dalkey, County Dublin
who died tragically at the age of 26.

# Priory Studios
Addicted to Photography

## The Family Portrait Photographers
## Celebrating 25 Years

# Priory Studios
## Addicted to Photography

**All photographs taken by Dominic Lee, AMPA**
except the photograph of The Satellite Generals at Burn Night Club taken by Shakira Lee
and the photograph of Dominic Lee on MV Ushuaia in Antarctica taken by Rob Lee

**Digital Design by Vladimir Polivanov, LBIPP**
"Out of Your Tree 2" Published by Priory Studios
Old Dublin Road, Stillorgan, Co. Dublin, Ireland
www.priorystudios.ie
Follow us on www.twitter.com/priorystudios
**ISBN 0-9524931-6-0**
Printed in Ireland by ColourBooks Ltd.
2009

# The Charity

The mission of the Irish Cancer Society, the national cancer care charity, is to play a vital role in achieving world-class cancer services in Ireland, to ensure fewer people get cancer and those who do have better outcomes. Our goals are focused around prevention, early detection and fighting cancer with three programme areas; advocacy, cancer services and research.

The Irish Cancer Society:

- runs nationwide cancer awareness, prevention and early detection campaigns to help people to reduce their risk of developing cancer;
- provides information and support to people with cancer and their families and friends;
- provides nursing care for people with cancer at the end stage of their cancer journey in their own homes;
- funds pre-clinical and clinical research in hospitals and universities across Ireland; and,
- advocates for the delivery of the National Cancer Control Strategy and the implementation of evidence-based policies and practices in the best interest of preventing cancer and of the people affected by cancer.

Cancer currently affects one in three people during the course of their lifetime in Ireland. The latest data from the National Cancer Registry of Ireland indicates that there were 27,930 cases of cancer diagnosed in 2007, with the Central Statistics Office recording 7,844 deaths from the disease. Furthermore, new cancer cases are expected to reach over 40,000 by the year 2020. This is largely due to an ageing and increasing population and a neglect of healthy lifestyle behaviours. However thanks to advances in cancer diagnosis and treatment, the prognosis is improving all of the time. Today more and more people who develop cancer go on to lead normal lives.

For information, advice and support on any aspect of cancer please call the National Cancer Helpline on Freefone 1800 200 700 and speak to a specialist nurse in confidence or visit www.cancer.ie.

# The Sponsors

Along with the generosity of the people who feature in the book, the following sponsors
helped to make it all possible by pre-ordering a quantity of books or by making a sizable contribution.

Noel & Kay Noonan
Dermot Desmond
Bruhenny Holdings Ltd (Gerry Murphy)
Peter & Derville Gleeson
Nikon
Moira & Bernard McNamara
Brenson Lawlor Accountants
Carmel Naughton
Sir Gerry & Lady Heather Robinson
BPP Professional Education
Landsdowne Hotel
Milltown Mosque (by an anonymous donor)
Paul Traynor
Eamon Hedderman Architects
Aidan Fitzgerald Hair Salon
Maeve & Donal Lydon
Gerard & Mary Duff
Sharp Design
Stillorgan Chamber of Commerce

Brian & Finula Goggin
Virgin Active (Richard Baker)
Michael & Carol Holland
Gleeson McGrath Baldwin
Susan & Nigel Spence
InternNational Ireland
Insure.ie
Dr Gerard O'Hare
Sean Gallagher
Google
Delpac
Edward Dillon & Co.
Spectrum Print Logistics
Cleaning Contactors
Rocwell Water
Denis O'Brien
Seamus Monahan & Partners
ColourBooks Ltd.
H.A.O'Neil Ltd

Please see the list of acknowledgments on the last page.

# Out of Your Tree 1

Here are a few examples from the first book which was a resounding success, enabling Priory Studios to donate €36,000 to The Central Remedial Clinic. The proceeds from Out of Your Tree 2 will be in aid of The Irish Cancer Society.

Roy Keane

Barry McGuigan

Sonny Condell

Diarmuid Gavin

Sharon Corr

Mike Murphy

Padraig Harrington

Norma Smurfit

Jimmy Magee

Adele King

Bertie Ahern

Sean McGinley

Peter Sheridan

Bernadette Greevy

Brian D'Arcy

Mathews

Dr Diarmuid Martin

Brendan Grace

# Out of Your Tree 2 - Introduction by Maeve Binchy

You never get to know people properly until you know what they do off-duty. That is why this selection of portraits by Dominic Lee is so special. Another picture of these subjects in a familiar setting would have been just that, another picture. Dominic's pictures open a door to a different side of a personality. Otherwise, who would have known what half these people might have chosen as a pastime?

Out of Your Tree 2 also lets us see a softer side, a more energetic side, a quirkier aspect and often an unexpected area of people's lives. But let me tell you that choosing a pose for such a picture is not always as easy as it might seem.

In my own case I have played chess happily every day for over 35 years with Gordon Snell. Amazingly we have invested all this time without either of us getting even remotely better at the game. Fortunately we are evenly matched, regarding it as an exciting game of chance where the cry "Oops there goes my Queen" is often heard. But the big problem for our particular photo shoot was not what to wear or how to smile, it was how to set out the chess board so that any REAL chess player looking at it would not be horrified and affronted and wondering how we had got ourselves into that particular position.

Dominic has captured the enthusiasms and eagerness of those he has photographed. It reminds me so much of a wonderful day in the convent school well over fifty years ago when we were allowed to ask the nuns one question each about their private lives before they entered Religion. Of course it had to be circumscribed a bit because boisterous teenage girls might have asked about sex and love and other unsuitable matters. We were allowed to ask them about their hobbies. I remember since the 1950s one elderly roly poly nun who said that hers was roller skating and we always checked out her shoes afterwards in case she had gone back to it.

Another thin faced angry looking nun said she loved making pastry and would create dishes that she might give to Lord Byron, if he ever came back to life, in order to comfort him and reassure him and take away his angst. We had no trouble in learning our English poetry after that.

If Dominic had been around in earlier times he might have photographed Henry the Eighth playing tennis, or James Joyce singing or Samuel Beckett teeing off for a game of golf. Undoubtedly he would have put them all at their ease and made the session seem painless and worthwhile.

Dominic is also raising money to help the Irish Cancer Society with the publication of this book. Indeed, what better reason to buy this book and browse through the faces of people doing what you would never expect them to be doing.

*Maeve Binchy*

# Liam Siffert

**Profession:**
Toddler (3 years old)

**Hobby:**
Sledging

**Favourite Quotation:**
"Ich bin der Erste!"

NB.
Liam featured on
the last page of the first
"Out of Your Tree" book
while still in his Mother's
tummy.

Markbachjoch, Niederau, Austria

# Aidan Fitzgerald

**Profession:**
Hairdresser

**Hobby:**
Cycling on tandem
bicycles with his wife
Karen, his son Ryan and
daughter Ruby Scarlett

**Favourite Quotation:**
"Think big and your deeds
will grow.
Think small and you'll
fall behind.
Think that you can and
you will.
It's all in a state of mind."

**NB.**
The Fitzgerald family had
this quote on a sampler
hanging in the family home
and it has passed from
generation to generation.

Glenart Gate Lodge, Woodenbridge, Co. Wicklow

# Cora Venus Lunny

**Profession:** Violinist     **Hobby:** Books

**Favourite Quotation:** "When you re-read a classic you do not see more in the book than you did before, you see more in you than there was before."

Clifton Fadiman

The Long Room, Trinity College, Dublin

# Amy
# Huberman

**Profession:**
Actor & Writer

**Hobby:**
Tilly, her Cavalier King
Charles Spaniel

**Favourite Quotation:**
"Through a chink too wide
there comes in no wonder."

Patrick Kavanagh

# Feargal Quinn

**Profession:**
Independent Senator

**Hobby:**
Brent Geese

**Favourite Quotation:**
"Éist le fuaim na h-abhann
is gheobhaidh tú bradán."
Seanfhoail

NB.
Shown here in Portmarnock
Golf Club watching the
October arrival of Brent
Geese, which return to
Canada in April. The Geese
are not very popular on Golf
Courses as their droppings
foul the greens.

Portmarnock, Co. Dublin

# His Excellency David Reddaway

**Profession:**
British Ambassador

**Hobby:**
Rowing

**Favourite Poem:**
"As one who, gazing at
a vista of beauty,
Sees the clouds close in
And turns his back in
sorrow, hearing
The thunderclaps begin,
So we, whose life was
all before us,
Our hearts with sunlight
filled,
Left in the hills our books
and flowers,
Descended and were killed.
Write on the stone no
words of sadness,
Only the gladness due
That we, who asked the
most of living,
Knew how to give it too."

Frank Thompson

NB.
"This poem means a lot
to me as it's by Frank
Thompson, who served with
my father in World War II
and was killed in action in
1944, aged 23."

River Liffey, Islandbridge, Dublin

# Rashan Reddaway

**Profession:**
Archaeologist &
Rare Plant Finder

**Hobby:**
Animals

**Favourite Quotation:**
"Good fortune is knotted
in the horses' forelocks
until the Day of Judgement,
and the horses' owners are
assisted in their care of
them, so stroke their
forelocks, and pray that
they be blessed."

Attributed to the Prophet
Muhammed & the Quar'an

Leopardstown, Co. Dublin

# Brian Kennedy

**Profession:** Singer      **Hobby:** Working out at the Gym
**Favourite Quotation:** "The only way to get rid of a temptation is to yield to it." Oscar Wilde

NB. Body Building is the only thing I can think of where FAILING is SUCCEEDING, pushing your muscle to the point of failure that is..!
Paul Byrne explained that to me and once I understood, it helped me get even more motivated. When I'm in the gym I can forget about
the world. Bodybuilding truly is an art form and it's never too late to transform your body, sure it's only water and flesh after all.

Bodybyrne Fitness, Dublin

# Dermot Earley

**Profession:**
Army Officer

**Hobby:**
Sport, especially Gaelic
Football and Hurling

**Favourite Quotation:**
"Attitude is more
important than ability,
Motive is more
important than method,
Courage is more
important than
cleverness and have
your heart in the right
place."

NB.
General Earley played for
Roscommon and his son
Dermot seen here on the
left, plays for Kildare.

St. Conleth's Park, Newbridge, Co. Kildare

**Borg Family**
**Profession:** Company Director
**Hobby:** Sailing
**Favourite Quotations:**

**Simone**
"Without friends no one would choose to live."

Aristotle

**Stanley**
"The best vision is insight."

Malcolm S. Forbes

**Sean**
"Life is like a box of chocolates: You never know what you're gonna get."

Forrest Gump - Movie

**Janice**
"The secret of a good life is to have the right loyalties and hold them in the right scale of values."

Norman Thomas

Kalkara, Malta

Malta

SEAJAN
PORT VICTORIA

# Sir Gerry Robinson

**Profession:**
TV Executive

**Hobby:**
Trains

**Favourite Quotation:**
"Nothing matters but the writing. There has been nothing else worthwhile. I couldn't have done it otherwise, gone on I mean. I could not have gone through the awful wretched mess of life without having left a stain upon the silence."

Samuel Beckett

NB.
Gerry runs a steam engine "The Duchess of Difflin" and a diesel engine "The Earl of Oakfield" over 3 km of railway track on his land in Raphoe.

Frost covered box-hedge at Gerry's train station, on a - 6°C January morning

Raphoe, Co. Donegal

The Music Room, Castlehyde, Co. Cork

## Michael Flatley

**Profession:**
Dancer

**Hobby:**
Playing & Collecting Flutes

**Favourite Quotation:**
"Nothing is impossible,
follow your dreams."

Beverly Hills, Los Angeles, California

# Peter J Gleeson

**Profession:** Businessman　　**Hobby:** Driving his Vintage Daimler
**Favourite Quotation:** "If a man does not make new acquaintances as he advances through life, he will soon find himself left alone. A man, sir, should keep his friendships in a constant repair." Samuel Johnson

NB. Peter's 1969 Daimler V8. 250 used to belong to his father William.

K Club, Co. Kildare

**City Girls**
**Profession:** Girls Group
**Hobby:** Boxing
**Favourite Quotations:**

**Sophie Leniston**
"Work hard, play hard."

**Rebecca Doran**
"Pain is temporary, glory is everlasting."

**Sian Charlesworth**
"Live as if you were to die tomorrow. Learn as if you were to live forever."

**Sheena Rowe**
"We all of us are stars and we all deserve to twinkle." Marilyn Monroe

Wednesbury Boxing Club, UK

# Bernard Dunne

**Profession:** Boxer     **Hobby:** Greyhound Racing
**Favourite Quotation:** "Ever tried. Ever failed. No matter. Try again. Fail better."   Samuel Beckett

NB. As we returned to the restaurant at Harold's Cross Race Track, some children asked Bernard for his autograph, Bernard asked them for a tip. One boy (about 8 yrs old) suggested his Dad's dog no.4, Bernard advised him that if it lost he would "come looking for him" to which the boy replied: "if you lose your next fight I'll come looking for you."

Harold's Cross Racing Track, Dublin

Rob Lee

**Profession:** Student          **Hobby:** Water Sports
**Favourite Quotation:** "Too many girls, not enough time."

Iguazu Falls, on the border of Brazil and Argentina

Plate River, Argentina

# Carmel Naughton

**Profession:**
Farmer

**Hobby:**
Beekeeping

**Favourite Poem:**

A Swarm of Bees Worth Having

B patient, B prayerful,
B humble, B mild,
B wise as a Solon,
B meek as a child;
B studious, B thoughtful,
B loving, B kind;
B sure you make matter
subservient to mind,
B cautious, B prudent,
B trustful, B true,
B courteous to all men,
B friendly with few,
B temperate in argument,
pleasure and wine,
B careful, B grateful,
B hopeful, B firm,
B peaceful, benevolent,
willing to learn;
B courageous, B gentle
B liberal, B just,
B aspiring, B humble,
because thou art dust;
B penitent, circumspect,
sound in the faith,
B active, devoted;
B faithful till death.
B honest, B holy,
transparent and pure;
B dependent, B Christ-like
and you'll B secure.

The Elyria Courier, 1850

Slane, Co.Meath

# Paul Brady

**Profession:** Singer & Songwriter　　　**Hobby:** Cooking

**Favourite Quotation:** "...be patient to all that is unsolved in your heart and try to love the questions themselves... like locked rooms and like books that are written in a very foreign tongue. Live the questions now... and for the rest, let life happen to you. Believe me: life is right, in any case."

Rainer Maria Rilke, 1903

Du

# Paulo Tullio

**Profession:**
Food Critic

**Hobby:**
Carpentry

**Favourite Quotation:**
"γνωθι σαυτον – nosci te ipsum - know yourself."
Attributed to Socrates

This is the start of the potting shed shown in the photograph opposite

Wicklow

# Dr Ali Al Saleh

**Profession:** Imam          **Hobby:** Vacuuming the Mosque
**Favourite Quotation:** "The master of the community is their servant." Prophet Muhammed

Quar'an at The Chester Beatty Library, Dublin Castle

Shia Mosque, Milltown, Co.Dublin

# Brent Pope

**Profession:**
Rugby Commentator

**Hobby:**
Writing Children's Books

**Favourite Quotation:**
"Imagination is more important than knowledge. Knowledge is limited. Imagination encircles the world."

Albert Einstein

Carysfort Park, Co. Dublin

# Margaret & Brendan Doherty

Profession: Retired Nurses     Hobby: Feeding the Swans on Lough Ennell
Favourite Quotations: "Love many, trust few,      "What whiskey will not cure,
                always paddle your own canoe."     there is no cure for."

Co.Westmeath

# Caroline Casey

**Profession:** Social Entrepreneur    **Hobby:** Elephants
**Favourite Quotation:** "All men dream: but not equally. Those who dream by night in the dusty recesses of their minds wake in the day to find that it was vanity: but the dreamers of the day are dangerous men, for they may act their dreams with open eyes, to make it possible."    T. E. Lawrence, The Seven Pillars of Wisdom

Dublin Zoo, Phoenix Park

# Charlie Nash

**Profession:** Boxer     **Hobby:** Snooker

**Favourite Quotation:** "He who is not courageous enough to take risks, will accomplish nothing in life."     Muhammed Ali

NB. Charlie is a former Irish, British and twice European Lightweight Champion.

Joyland Snooker Centre, Derry

# Anna Stepunina & Vitaly Sevastijanov

**Profession:** Latin American Dancers    **Hobby:** Cats
**Favourite Quotation:** "Ibi Victoria, Ubi Concordia." (Victory is there where there is consent)

NB. Vitaly & Anna met while dancing, they recently got married and are currently the All Ireland Latin Dance Champions.

Baileys & Ozi

Dublin

# His Exellency Urabe

**Profession:**
Japanese Ambassador

**Hobby:**
Scubadiving

**Favourite Quotation:**
"The way to get things done is not to mind who gets the credit for doing them."

Benjamin Jowlett

NB.
Ambassador Urabe has extensive experience in diving in tropical seas all around the world.
He obtained his diving licence in Sri Lanka and has dived many times in the Maldives.
"The beauty of these seas is not only the visibility that allows you to see many things, but also the fact that one doesn't have to wear clumsy wetsuits! One just gets on a boat, jumps off and drift dives. One can see beautiful corals, tropical fish and occasionally manta rays and sharks."

Dublin

# Chips Chipperfield

**Profession:** Film Producer (Beatles Anthology)      **Hobby:** Calling the Corncrake
**Favourite Quotation:** "Someday this will all be a long long time ago."   Marcel Marceau

NB. Birdwatchers use two serrated bones to imitate the crek-crek sound of the Corncrake, a rapidly dwindling species, high on the conservation list.

Dingle, Co. Kerry

# David Norris

**Profession:**
Independent Senator

**Hobby:**
Playing the Piano

**Favourite Quotation:**
"Judge not another till you have stood in his shoes."

Rabbi Ben Ezra of Cairo

NB.
The reflection in the brass sign is David's Georgian house, which is opposite the James Joyce Centre in North Great George's St.

Dublin

# Darina Allen

**Profession:**
Chef

**Hobby:**
Chickens

**Favourite Quotation:**
"Happiness is a wine of
the rarest vintage and
seems insipid to a vulgar
taste."

Loga Pearsall Smith

NB.
The octagonal Shell
House at the rear of the
herbaceous garden has
its interior beautifully
decorated with sea
shells from cockles,
mussels, scallops and
oysters by Charlotte
Kerr Wilson. See extra
photo on the back page.

Ballymaloe, Shanagarry, Co.Cork

# Chris Hudson, MBE

**Profession:** Church Minister **Hobby:** Lead Soldiers
**Favourite Quotation:** "Though I speak with the tongues of men and of angels, and have not love, I am become as sounding brass, or a tinkling cymbal. And though I have the gift of prophecy, and understand all mysteries, and all knowledge; and though I have all faith, so that I could remove mountains, and have not love, I am nothing." 13: 1 to 2

Blackrock, Co. Dublin

# Ciaran Forbes

**Profession:** Member of Glenstal Abbey Benedictine Community      **Hobby:** Turning Wood

**Favourite Quotation:** " You are one of Nature's thoughts and they are all wise."   Karen Blixen

NB. Shown here with his beloved companion Bede, surrounded by a variety of timbers from which he has produced bowls over the last forty years.

Glenstal Abbey, Co Limerick

# Ann Marie Nohl

**Profession:**
Restaurateur

**Hobby:**
Horse Riding with
her daughter Sara

**Favourite Quotation:**
"Change will not come if
we wait for some other
person or some other time.
We are the ones we've
been waiting for...we are
the change we seek."
Barack Obama

Sara riding Bruce at Tom Atlin's Stables, Kilternan, Dublin

# Dara Hogan

**Profession:** Chartered Management Accountant     **Hobby:** Paragliding

**Favourite Quotation:** "We don't stop playing because we grow old - we grow old because we stop playing."    George Bernard Shaw

NB. Dara has been paragliding with his son, Eoin, since 1995 and he is the chairman of the Irish Hang Gliding & Paragliding Association. He has logged 280 hours and has flown abroad in France, Spain, Italy, Austria, Slovakia, Turkey and Morocco.

Mount Leinster, on the Carlow/Wexford border

# Brian Goggin

**Profession:**
Banker

**Hobby:**
Barbecuing

**Favourite Quotation:**
"You only get out of
life what you are
prepared to put in."

Dublin

# Declan O'Rourke

**Profession:** Singer & Songwriter          **Hobby:** Exploring the Antarctic (from his couch)
**Favourite Quotation:** "Every man has to seek in his own way, to make his own self more noble and to realise his own true worth."          Albert Schweitzer

A Wandering Albatross on Prion Island and the ship MV Ushuaia in the Bay of Isles

Killarney, Co. Kerry

# Jack Kyle

**Profession:** Retired Doctor and Rugby Player          **Hobby:** Collecting Wooden Carvings
**Favourite Quotation:** "In this world there are only two tragedies; one is not getting what one wants, and the other is getting it."   Oscar Wilde

Newcastle, Co. Down

# Tara
# Leniston

**Profession:**
Actor

**Hobby:**
Martial Arts

**Favourite Quotation:**
"You don't love a woman
because she is beautiful;
she is beautiful because
you love her."

Grace Kelly

NB.
Tara met Jackie Chan
while living in Hong Kong,
he introduced her to
martial arts. She starred
in his film The Medallion.

Clontarf, Co. Dublin

## Dermot O'Neill

**Profession:**
Gardener

**Hobby:**
Singing

**Favourite Quotation:**
"If one is the master of one thing and understands one thing well, one has at the same time insight into and understanding of many things."

Vincent Van Gogh

RTE Concert Orchestra, Dublin

# Francie Conway

**Profession:**
Musician

**Hobby:**
Fly-fishing with
his son, Rory

**Favourite Quotation:**
"All you need is Love."

John Lennon

NB.
Rory is a very special child,
who contracted meningitis
when he was two and a half
years old and after eight
major brain operations,
his family refer to him as
The Miracle Boy. See extra
photo on the back page.

River Liffey, Manor Kilbride, Co. Wicklow

# Derry Clarke

**Profession:** Chef & Restaurateur      **Hobby:** Boating

**Favourite Quotation:** " The mind is like an iceberg - it floats with only one-seventh of its bulk above water." Sigmund Freud

Derry with his son Andrew in Dun Laoghaire Harbour

Dun Laoghaire Marina

# Colette Fitzpatrick

**Profession:**
TV Presenter

**Hobby:**
Wine Appreciation

**Favourite Poem:**
Had I the heavens'
embroidered cloths,
Enwrought with golden
and silver light,
The blue and the dim
and the dark cloths
Of night and light and
the half-light,
I would spread the cloths
under your feet:
But I, being poor,
have only my dreams;
I have spread my dreams
under your feet;
Tread softly because
you tread on my dreams.

W.B. Yeats

Wine Cellar in Luca, Italy

Colette with her sister Olivia

# Dominic Lee

**Profession:**
Photographer

**Hobby:**
Seeing the World

**Favourite Quotation:**
"Observe the masses and do the opposite."

NB.
Since the age of 18, Dominic has travelled to 45 countries around the world.

P.S. "I awoke at 3 am shivering with the cold and while out walking I watched this penguin approach the tent, he stopped and stared at it as if to say - that was not here yesterday." See extra photo on the back page.

Dorian Bay, Antarctica

Glacier in Drygalski Fjord, Antarctica.

# Dermot Desmond

**Profession:** Investor    **Hobby:** Golf

**Favourite Quotation:** "To laugh often and much; to win the respect of intelligent people and the affection of children; to earn the appreciation of honest critics and endure the betrayal of false friends; to appreciate beauty; to find the best in others; to leave the world a bit better; whether by a child, a garden patch, or a redeemed social condition; to know even one life has breathed easier because you lived; this is to have succeeded." Bessie Stanley

Dublin

# Dr Hubie O'Connor

**Profession:**
Gynaecologist

**Hobby:**
Oil Painting

**Favourite Quotation:**
"It's four in the morning-
she's ready!"

NB.
Dr O'Connor has written
the autobiography of
Dr Barry E.O'Meara, who
was Napoleon's doctor on
the Isle of St. Helena.

Dublin

# Fíodhna Campbell

**Profession:**
Student

**Hobby:**
Irish Dancing

**Favourite Quotation:**
"Dance is the hidden language of the soul."
Martha Graham

NB.
The love of Fíodhna's life is equally divided between Irish dancing and horse riding.

Ballinaclash, Co. Wicklow

Ceiling of St. John's Co-Cathedral

# Donal Lydon

**Profession:**
Consulting Psychologist and President of the Association of Papal Orders in Ireland

**Hobby:**
Orders of Chivalry

**Favourite Quotation:**
"The things you now refuse will not be offered again in all eternity."

Friedrich Von Shiller

NB.
The Order of Malta is The Sovereign Military Hospitaller Order of St. John of Jerusalem, of Rhodes and Malta.

St. John's Co-Cathedral, Valletta, Malta

# Frank Quinn

Profession: Publican & Hotelier        Hobby: Hill Walking (shown here crossing South Georgia in the footsteps of Shackleton, Crean & Wolsey)
Favourite Quotation: "Níl aon tinteán mar do thinteán féin."

NB. Frank has also been trekking in Camino de Santiago - Spain, The Drakensberg Mountains - South Africa, Macchu Piccu - Peru, Chiang Mai - Thailand, The Grand Canyon - USA, Mount Kilimanjaro - Tanzania and Everest Annapurna - Nepal.

Frank (10th from left) decending into Fortuna Bay, South Georgia

Stromness Whaling Station, South Georgia

# Noirín
# Ní Riain

**Profession:**
Singer

**Hobby:**
Stone Circles

**Favourite Quotation:**
"All shall be well,
all shall be well and
all manner of things
shall be well."

Julian of Norwich

NB.
The stone circle at Grange is
the largest and finest in
Ireland. It was built about
2,100 BC by Bronze Age
people living around the lake.
Grange Stone Circle is
almost certainly a religious
site. We know nothing of the
rituals which began here over
4,000 years ago, but they
may well have been held at
dawn on midsummer's
morning. As the sun rises,
the first rays of light shine
directly through the narrow
entrance passageway and
into the centre of the circle.

Grange Stone Circle near Lough Gur, Limerick

# Sir Hugh Orde, OBE

**Profession:** President of The Association of Chief Police Officers (former Chief Constable of the PSNI)  **Hobby:** Vintage Tractors
**Favourite Quotation:** "Trust is good, supervision is better."

NB. Sir Hugh received this tractor from his partner for his 50th birthday. He worked on a farm prior to joining
the Metropolitan Police and drove a very similar tractor. It now has vintage status.

Belfast

# Frank Brady

**Profession:**
Maxillofacial Surgeon

**Hobby:**
Vintage Coins

**Favourite Quotation:**
"Experience is the
name everyone gives
to their mistakes."
Oscar Wilde

Dublin

# Sir John Leslie

**Profession:**
Owner of Castle Leslie

**Hobby:**
Antiques

**Favourite Quotation:**
"He who laughs last,
laughs best (I am still
waiting to laugh last)."

NB.
"The fireplace is by the
famous Florentine sculptor
Andrea Della Robbia
(1437-1528). It dates from
about 1490. The priests
at the church of Santa
Maria Novella in Florence
were selling it as they
wished to substitute it with
a new marble one over an
altar. My great grandfather
bought it about 1875."

Castle Leslie, Co. Monaghan

# Satellite Generals

**Profession:**
Students

**Hobby:**
Playing Music

**Favourite Quotations:**

## Jamie Duff
"The great thing about music is, that when it hits you, it doesn't hurt."

Bob Marley

## Niall Rogers
"Heard melodies are sweet, but those unheard are sweeter."

John Keats

## James Rogers
When asked if Ringo was the best drummer in the world, John Lennon said "Ringo isn't even the best drummer in the Beatles."

## Graham O'Hara
"And you can function as someone besides who you are."

John Frusciante

Burn Night Club, Dublin

Dublin

# Thelma Mansfield

**Profession:** Artist & TV Presenter          **Hobby:** Kitchen Memorabilia
**Favourite Quotation:** "He who works with his hands is a labourer, he who works with his hands and his head is a craftsman.
He who works with his hands and his head and his heart is an artist." St. Francis of Assisi

Glenageary, Co. Dublin

# John Morris

**Profession:**
Photographer

**Hobby:**
Falconry

**Favourite Quotation:**
"One hawk one wife
two hawks no wife!"

Dublin

# Karen Conway

**Profession:**
Media Planner and Buyer

**Hobby:**
Hammer Throwing

**Favourite Quotation:**
"Reach for the moon,
if you fall short you will
land on a star."

NB.
Hammer throwing has its
origins in the ancient
Tailteann Games, that took
place on the Hill of Tara,
County Meath. It has
evolved into an Olympic
sport with Irish born
athletes winning the first
five Olympiads in the event.
The event requires speed
and technique, there are
different weights for age
and the person who throws
the furthest wins. The event
combines swinging the
hammer around the head
before a heel turn into
rotations which project the
hammer into a throw.

UCD Belfield, Dublin

# Kevin
# Dundon

**Profession:**
Chef & Hotelier

**Hobby:**
Skiing

**Favourite Quotation:**
"My mom offered two
dishes: take it or leave it."

NB.
Kevin took up skiing two
years ago and will never
do a sun holiday again!

Markbachjoch, Niederau, Austria

St. Anton, Austria

# John Murray

**Profession:** Chief Justice of Ireland
**Hobby:** Antique Irish Silver

**Favourite Poem:** Upon a headland by a whinny hedge
A hare sits looking down a leaf-lapped furrow
There's an old plough upside-down on a weedy ridge
And someone is shouldering home a saddle-harrow.
Out of that childhood country what fools climb
To fight with tyrants Love and Life and Time? Patrick Kavanagh

John holding a collector's piece: Loving Cup by Joseph Johns, Limerick c.1760

Wicklow

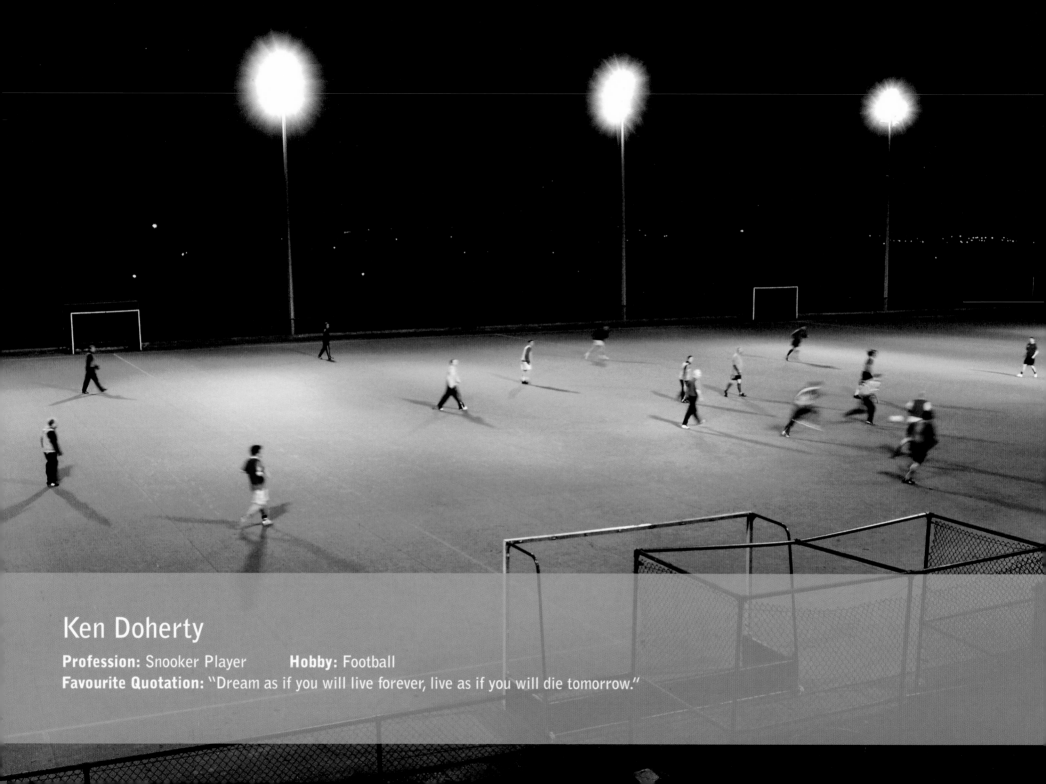

# Ken Doherty

**Profession:** Snooker Player     **Hobby:** Football
**Favourite Quotation:** "Dream as if you will live forever, live as if you will die tomorrow."

St. Columba's College, Rathfarnham, Co. Dublin

GAIETY
THEATRE
PLAZA
DECEMBER 2000

HANDPRINTS OF THE STARS
OF THE
GAIETY THEATRE
BOTH PAST AND PRESENT

Rosaleen Linehan

Anna Manahan

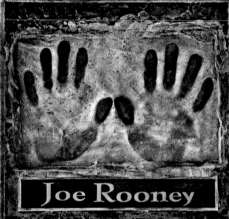

Joe Rooney

Luciano Pavarotti

Des Keogh

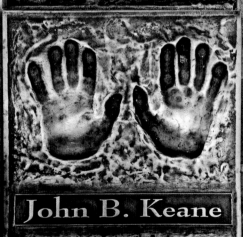

John B. Keane

Ronnie Drew

Milo O' Shea

# Luan Parle

**Profession:**
Singer

**Hobby:**
Live Comedy

**Favourite Quotation:**
"The hardest challenge is to be yourself in a world where everyone is trying to make you be somebody else."

E.E Cummings

NB.
Luan has had major chart success with her single "Ghost" and her album "Free" in 2008. She has also won the Meteor "Best Female Artist", Tatler "Music Woman of the Year", Balcony TV "Best Female Artist" and the Big Buzz "Best Female Performer" awards.

Dublin

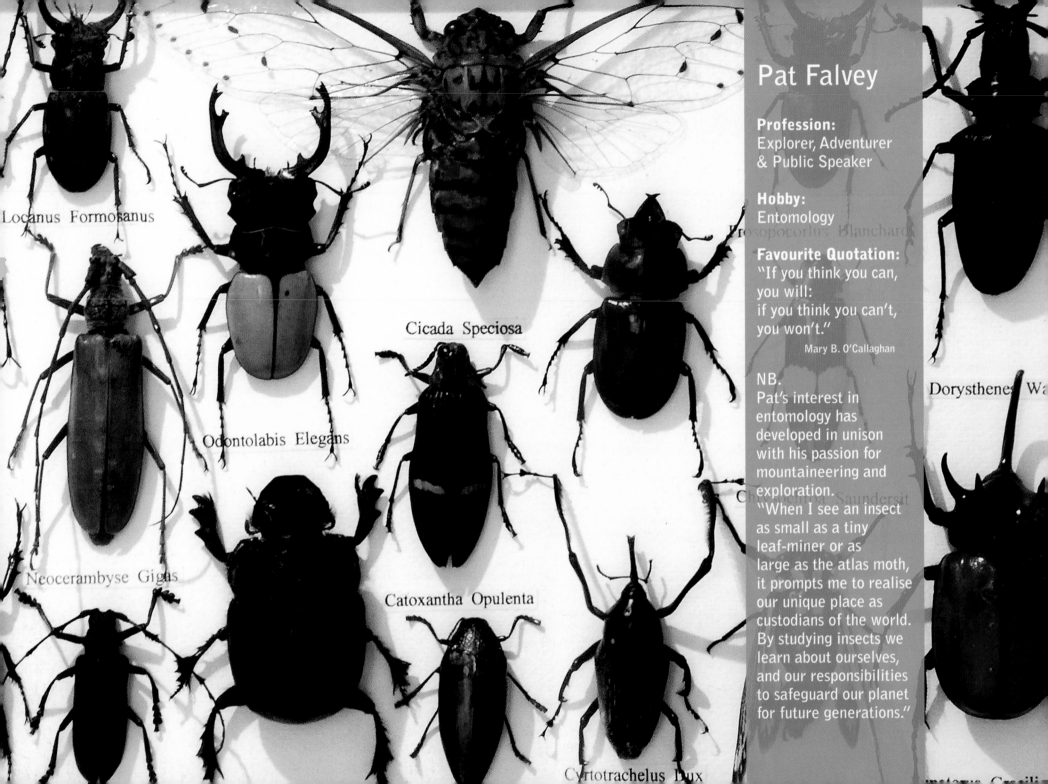

Locanus Formosanus

Odontolabis Elegans

Cicada Speciosa

Neocerambyse Gigas

Catoxantha Opulenta

Cyrtotrachelus Dux

Dorysthenes Wa

## Pat Falvey

**Profession:**
Explorer, Adventurer
& Public Speaker

**Hobby:**
Entomology

**Favourite Quotation:**
"If you think you can,
you will:
if you think you can't,
you won't."

Mary B. O'Callaghan

NB.
Pat's interest in
entomology has
developed in unison
with his passion for
mountaineering and
exploration.
"When I see an insect
as small as a tiny
leaf-miner or as
large as the atlas moth,
it prompts me to realise
our unique place as
custodians of the world.
By studying insects we
learn about ourselves,
and our responsibilities
to safeguard our planet
for future generations."

Killarney, Co. Kerry

# Linda Keating

**Profession:**
Director of the Marie Keating Foundation

**Hobby:**
Motor Racing

**Favourite Quotation:**
"The fear is in participating and I am glad when it's over and I am still a winner."

NB.
Following their mother Marie's death in 1998, each member of the Keating family promised that they would do everything they could to bring an end to breast cancer. They committed to provide all women and their families with the necessary information to prevent cancer or detect it at its earliest stages. Their collective aim was "enlighten not frighten." Through three mobile units the Foundation's dedicated nurses have enlightened almost 85,000 people of the causes and risk factors of breast and other cancers.
"Men Keeping Fit" is now a successful annual campaign and has significantly raised awareness among men of testicular and prostate cancer.

Mondello Park, Co. Kildare

# Maurice Gilbert

**Profession:**
Company Director

**Hobby:**
Restoring Castle Pook

**Favourite Quotation:**
"Hold tightly to the magic of the past for the present is the history of our future."

NB.
The Castle and its legends about the pooka may be the source of the name Puck, which Shakespeare gave the spirit Robin Goodfellow in "A Midsummer Night's Dream". The poet Edmund Spenser lived in Kilcolman, just three miles away from Castle Pook. He knew the castle and the legends attached to it (more, he was involved with lawsuits against the Synons who owned the castle). Spenser introduced the word "pook" to the English in his poem, The Epithalamium - "ne let the Pook, nor other evil sprites... Pray us with things that not be" - which he wrote to mark his marriage, and which first appeared in early 1595. English scholars acknowledge that Shakespeare took Puck from Spenser's Pook.

Castle Pook, Doneraile, Co. Cork

# Lisa Fitzpatrick

**Profession:**
TV & Radio Fashion
Presenter

**Hobby:**
Collecting Shoes

**Favourite Quotation:**
"The secret of success
is this: there is no
secret to success."

Elbert Hubbard

NB.
Lisa started her love affair
with shoes when she was
a size 18. Fed up buying
clothes which really would
not fit and with larger size
clothes being very old
fashioned at the time, she
would add colour-alert
through her shoes.

Minnie Peters Interior Design, Dublin

Kim, Sheva and Roxy at Butler's Quay, Clifden, Co. Galway

# Noel Noonan

**Profession:**
Retired Chairman of
Support Services Co.

**Hobby:**
Breeding Connemara
Ponies

**Favourite Quotation:**
"You can achieve
anything, God willing."

Noel with Ali and Dusty at Ardbear, Clifden, Co. Galway

# Lord O'Neill

**Profession:**
Company Director

**Hobby:**
Steam Trains

**Favourite Poem:**
"Gaily into Ruislip Gardens
Runs the red electric train,
with a thousand
Ta's and Pardon's
Daintily alights Elaine."

John Betjeman

NB.
John Betjeman was also
a Railway Enthusiast and
an acquaitance of Lord
Raymond O'Neill.

Whitehead, Co. Antrim

## Maeve Binchy

Profession:
Author & Novelist

Hobby: Chess

Favourite Quotation:
"You always regret the
things that you didn't do
in life, rather than the
things you did."

Mark Twain

## Gordon Snell

Profession: Writer of
Childrens Books & Comedy

Hobby: Chess

Favourite Quotation:
"What is this life if, full
of care, we have no time
to stand and stare?"

W. H. Davies

Dalkey Castle

Dalkey, Co. Dublin

# Michael Holland

**Profession:**
Entrepreneur

**Hobby:**
High Latitude Sailing

**Favourite Poem:**
"I read of a man who
stood to speak
At the funeral of a friend
He referred to the dates
on his tombstone
From the beginning to
the end.
He noted that first came
the date of his birth
And spoke the following
date with tears,
But he said what matters
most of all,
Was the dash between
those years.
For it matters not how
much we own, the cars,
the house, the cash,
What matters is how
we live and love and how
we spend our dash."

Linda Ellis

NB.
Michael was awarded
Ireland's most prestigious
adventure sailing award by
the Irish Cruising Club for
his voyage from the Arctic
to the Antarctic in 2008.

Michael sailing the 72 ft. Celtic Spirit of Fastnet with his daughter Sofie and son Michael at Fastnet Rock, Schull, Co. Cork.

## Robert Doggett

**Profession:** Restaurateur      **Hobby:** Theatre
**Favourite Quotation:** "Life is not a spectacle or a feast; it is a predicament."   George Santayana

Olympia Theatre, Dublin

# Norah Casey

**Profession:** Magazine Publisher       **Hobby:** Wildlife

**Favourite Quotation:** "Well behaved women seldom make history."   Laurel Thatcher Ulrich

NB. Norah was raised in a gate lodge in the Phoenix Park and so has a lasting affection for its wildlife, especially the graceful Fallow Deer who have lived in the Park since the 17th century.

January 2009

Phoenix Park, Dublin

# Paddy Goodwin

**Profession:** Solicitor      **Hobby:** Collecting Guitars
**Favourite Quotation:** "Wise men speak because they have something to say, fools because they have to say something."

The Bridge of Peace, Drogheda, Co. Louth

# Rotimi Adabari

**Profession:**
Mayor of Portlaoise

**Hobby:**
Tennis

**Favourite Quotation:**
"Lesser minds think of persons. Ordinary minds think of events but serious minds think of ideas because ideas build the world."

NB.
Rotimi was the first black person to be elected a Mayor in Ireland. He was elected to Portlaoise Town Council in 2004 and in June 2007 he was elected the Mayor of the town. He is origianally from Nigeria and has lived in Portlaoise with his family since 2000.

Deer Park Tennis Club, Mount Merrion, Co. Dublin

## Paul Harrington

**Profession:** Singer & Songwriter          **Hobby:** VW Beetles

**Favourite Quotation:** "It doesn't matter who you love or how you love, but that you love."   Rod McKuen

Dublin

81-D-2095

BAILE ÁTHA CLIATH

IRL

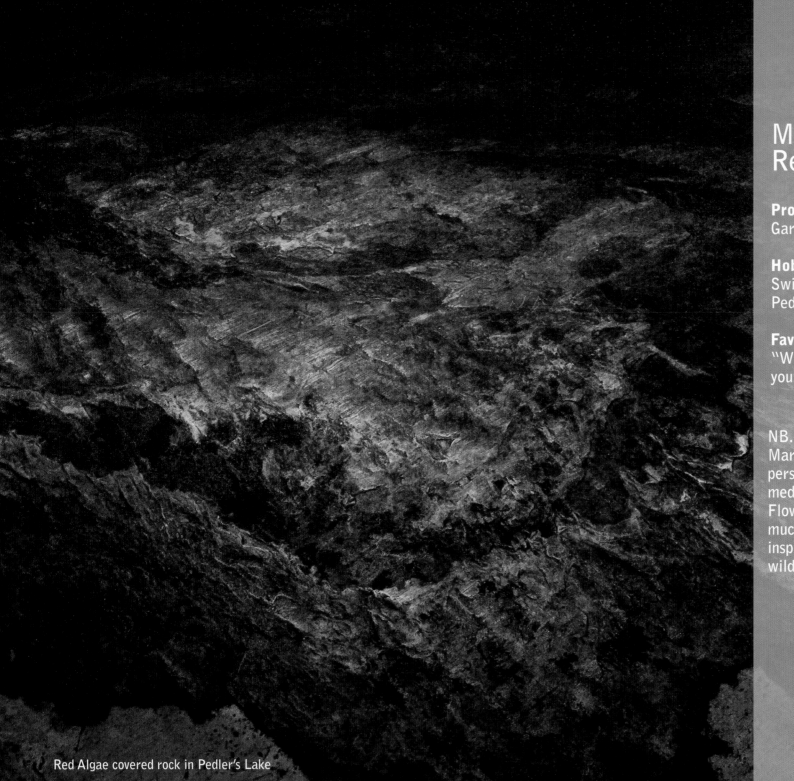

Red Algae covered rock in Pedler's Lake

# Mary Reynolds

**Profession:**
Garden Designer

**Hobby:**
Swimming in
Pedler's Lake

**Favourite Quotation:**
"What you think,
you become."

Buddah

NB.
Mary is the first Irish
person to win a gold
medal at the Chelsea
Flower Show. She finds
much of her design
inspiration from the
wild landscape of Kerry.

Conor Pass, Dingle, Co. Kerry

# Sir Richard Branson

**Profession:** Entrepreneur       **Hobby:** Kite Surfing

**Favourite Quotation:** "Nothing ventured, nothing gained!"

NB.  Richard re-introduced Flamingos to the Caribbean, which had disappeared from the region some 50 years ago.
This flamingo was feeding nearby. It would take off, flying in circles every time Richard approached. See extra photo on the back page.

Necker Island, Caribbean

Igls Bobsleighing Run, Austria

# His Excellency Richard Ryan

**Profession:**
Irish Ambassador to
the Netherlands

**Hobby:**
Korean Archery

**Favourite Quotation:**
"Tragedy is
underdeveloped comedy,
comedy not fully born."

Patrick Kavanagh

NB.
Richard took up his
hobby while serving as
Ambassador to the Republic
of Korea in 1989. He was
honoured with the
Seok-Ho-Jeong Award
of the Korean Archery
Association in 1993. The
traditional Korean bow is
made from horn-cherry
bark and magnolia and then
bound with fish glue. It has
an effective target range
of one hundred and fifty
meters and a maximum
range of six hundred
meters, double that
of the English Longbow.

The Hague, Holland

# Carol Cronin

**Profession:** Artist          **Hobby:** Surfing
**Favourite Quotation:** "Happiness depends upon ourselves."          Aristotle

NB. Carol is particularly well known for her wild seascapes.

Strandhill, Sligo

# Richard Baker

**Profession:** Company Chairman    **Hobby:** Playing Hockey
**Favourite Quotation:** "It may be the taking part that counts.... but the beer tastes better when you win!"

Bourne 3rds v St. Ives 4ths at Market Deeping, Lincolnshire, UK

The River Shannon

# Vard Sisters

**Profession:**
Singers

**Hobby:**
Cruising on
the Shannon

**Favourite Quotations:**

## Wendy
"What doesn't kill us only
makes us stronger."

## Lisa
"What's meant to be,
will be."

## Cathy
"Let go and let God."

NB.
The Vard family have had
a boat on the Shannon for
forty years.

Athlone, Co. Westmeath

Ronan Ó Snodaigh

**Profession:** Musician    **Hobby:** Dry Stone Wall Building
**Favourite Quotation:** "Dead fish go with the flow." Roy Keane

Dingle, Co. Kerry

# Paul Howard
(aka Ross O'Carroll-Kelly)

**Profession:**
Writer

**Hobby:**
Star Wars Memorabilia

**Favourite Quotation:**
"You can't win. Strike me
down and I shall become
more powerful than you
can possibly imagine."

Obi Wan Kenobi

NB.
Paul Howard has been
collecting Star Wars
Memorabilia for over thirty
years. He denies that this
makes him a nerd.

Wicklow

# Páidí Ó Sé

**Profession:**
Publican & six times
All Ireland Football
Medal Winner

**Hobby:**
Walking on Ventry Beach

**Favourite Quotation:**
"But what is happiness
except the simple harmony
between a man and the
life he leads?"

Albert Camus

NB.
Paudie's pub is in the
foreground, next to the
church.

Dingle Peninsula, Co. Kerry

# Sean Boyd

**Profession:** Student          **Hobby:** Acting

**Favourite Quotation:** "Live as if you were to die tomorrow. Learn as if you were to live forever."   Mahatma Gandhi

NB. Sean auditioned for the "Joseph and the Amazing Technicolor Dreamcoat" production by the Transition year students in Oatlands College and Sion Hill. He played Joseph in his first ever stage performance.

Oatlands College Hall, Stillorgan, Co.

# Ronan Flood

**Profession:**
Professional Golf Caddy

**Hobby:**
Blackjack

**Favourite Quotation:**
"I have failed many times,
that is why I'm a success."

Michael Jordan

Sporting Emporium, Dublin

## Judith Woodworth

**Profession:**
Director of The National
Concert Hall, Dublin

**Hobby:**
Gardening

**Favourite Poem:**
Had I the heavens'
embroidered cloths,
Enwrought with golden
and silver light,
The blue and the dim
and the dark cloths
Of night and light and
the half-light,
I would spread the cloths
under your feet:
But I, being poor,
have only my dreams;
I have spread my dreams
under your feet;
Tread softly because
you tread on my dreams.

W.B. Yeats

Blackrock, Co. Dublin

# Stuart McGrath

**Profession:**
Stone Mason

**Hobby:**
Mountain Biking

**Favourite Quotation:**
"Twenty years from now you will be more disappointed by the things you didn't do than by the ones you did. So throw off the bowlines, sail away from the safe harbour. Catch the trade winds in your sails. Explore, Dream!"

Mark Twain

Ticknock, Dublin Mountains

# Róisín Ingle

**Profession:**
Journalist

**Hobby:**
Karaoke

**Favourite Quotation:**
"We write our own
destiny... we become
what we do."

Madam Chiang Kai-Shek

WHEN YOU'RE ALONE
AND LIFE IS MAKING YOU
LONELY
YOU CAN ALWAYS GO
DOWNTOWN

Dublin

# Klara
# Chowanska

**Profession:**
Baby (age 5 months)

**Hobby:**
Flower Arranging

**Favourite Quotation:**
"da da."

Jack Leslie

Flamingo on Necker Island - Sir Richard Branson

The Spirit of Fastnet - Michael Holland

Caroline Casey

Rory Conway

Camping in Antarctica - Dominic Lee

The Shell House - Darina Allen

Noel Noonan

Sir Gerry Robinson

# The Back Page

These photographs were also contenders
for inclusion in the book.

Rob Lee

Cora Venus Lunny

Tara Leniston

Michael Flatley

Klara Chowanska

Fallow deer in The Phoenix Park - Norah Casey

# Acknowledgments

Many thanks for the kind permission and assistance afforded me at the many locations used in this book which are listed on the photographs.

I am also grateful to all those who suggested people to photograph, corrected spelling,
critiqued photographs, pre-ordered books or offered assistance, especially the following:

Judith Woodworth - The National Concert Hall
Maeve Binchy
Brian Reddin
Reelgood Recording Studios
Phelim Drew
Dunnes Stores
Stillorgan Shopping Centre
Joe Harrington - East Coast FM
Maggie French
Padraic & Sonia Deasy
Gerry & Dorothy Murphy
Mark Nixon
Sharp Design
Door-to-Door Distributors
Gerard Lee
Reads Print & Design
Oatlands College
Sisslings Mouldings
Priory Stores Newsagents
Tony Maddox
Norma Smurfit

Frank Murphy
Marjorie Courtney
Fergal & Sveta Megannety
Paul Lee
Justyna Borowska
Manuel Ryan
Crystal Holidays
DML
John & Tina Riordan
Brian Terry
Alan Kelly - Gentlemen Please
Luxuryweddingcars.ie
Linda Burke
Harmony Legrand
Kopikat
Prof Aidan Moran
Padraig MacGreil
Kamila & Alan Lyons
Tedcastles Lubricants
Michael McKay
The Irish Cancer Society

Thank you to the Staff at Priory Studios - Mairead, Linda, Sonny and Vladimir and the many girls who joined us
on work experience who were constantly called upon for their valued opinion with the selection from each photo shoot.

An extra special thanks to my daughter Shakira and son Rob for their continued love and enthusiastic support and to
my wife Mairead who chauffeured me around Ireland - North, South, East & West but was never able to accompany
me on the more exotic trips to Argentina, Antarctica, The Caribbean, Austria, Holland, England, Malta, and America.

*Dominic Lee*

## Competition

Win a €100 Voucher towards a Family Portrait at Priory Studios.

Answer ten questions, five shown here and the remaining five on www.priorystudios.ie/outofyourtree2

Winners will be notified by phone

Find the following in images or text:

     (1) Infinate Space

     (2) The Earl of Oakfield

     (3) Bacchus

     (4) Grace Kelly

     (5) Mayor O'Driscoll

# Priory Studios
### Addicted to Photography

## The Family Portrait Photographers
## Celebrating 25 Years

# Autographs